Ink & Insomnia

Scribbles in the Midnight Musings

- Prakhar Gupta

To Yuvraj and Akshita.

My personal banks that take no interest on my loans.

By The Way

A lot of people ask me, "Prakhar, how did you come up with all these ideas? ***Where does the inspiration come from?****"*

Well, to be honest, the short answer is: it just comes. Sometimes it's late-night scribbles that start as random thoughts, and other times, it's the conversations I have with my friends that spark something new. But one thing I can tell you is, it's never planned. Art doesn't follow a schedule, and neither do my ideas.

When I started writing this book, I didn't have a goal in mind—except maybe to make people think. But as I kept jotting down my thoughts, I realized something: each line, each quote, was a reflection of who I am and where I've been. I didn't want to create something that was just nice to read; I wanted to make something that would resonate with you. You know, something that'll make you say, "Wah! Kya sahi baat boli hai."

If you're reading this, chances are you're looking for something real. Something that's not just a quick scroll on your phone but a piece of content that makes you stop, think, and even share with others. This is a book that you'll pick up at cafe and get lost in, then maybe post a line on your Instagram story because, let's be honest, it's too good to keep to yourself.

So, whether you're here for the quotables or you're just wondering how many pages you need to get through before you start feeling like it's worth it (trust me, you'll want to finish a book that takes less than 30 minutes to complete),

this book is for you.

And hey, if any line hits you, don't forget to tag me. ***You know the drill! Make some noise!***

- Prakhar Gupta

Before We Begin

'Jinhe Padhna Chahiye,

Wo Likh Rahe Hain'

("Those who should be reading,

are busy writing.")

- Jaun Elia

This line really resonated with me. While writing this book, it kept running through my mind repeatedly. By profession, I'm an artist—a rapper, to be precise—and writing is my craft. Jaun Elia's words remind me of a line from my own rap, "Cheen Lunga":

"Ye kal ke ladke chhode school karne follow rap,

Mai bhi hu rapper fir bhi chhodi na padhayi maine"

After finishing school, I started preparing for NEET under societal pressure, but my heart refused to drift away from hip-hop. Eventually, I quit NEET preparation and dedicated myself to exploring the artistic field full-time.

I was good at studies, and perhaps that's why not having something to read always felt strange. Even today, I carry a notebook and a poetry book in my bag. Yes, you'll always find me with a bag—without it, it feels like I'm missing a part of myself. Though I left school, school never left me.

I read different books, jot down what I learn, and get inspired to write notes, one-liners, raps, and more.

In short, ***Hum padh bhi rahe hain aur likh bhi rahe hain.***

(we're reading and writing both).

This book is a compilation of quotables, Shayari, and one-liners—handpicked late-night thoughts that carry deep meanings and will make you reflect. Our generation lacks the patience to read thoroughly. They prefer scrolling on their phones instead. Books, for most, are props to add aesthetics to their Instagram and Snapchat stories (not judging, I do that too. Hehe).

So, I've designed this book in a way that you can simply snap a photo of what you like and post it on your social media story.

If you're reading these long pages, salute to you!

And yeah, if any page from this book makes it to your story, don't forget to **mention me (@prakharleo8)**—
I'd love to know what you liked and why you liked it.

A Note of Thanks

"I wanna thank me, for believing in me. I wanna thank me for doing all this hard work. I wanna thank me for having no days off."

- Snoop Dogg

Hehe... just kidding. There are so many people I want to thank—people whose actions, knowingly or unknowingly, led me here, making me confident enough to publish this book.

For starters, Vaibhav, with whom I began my original writing journey. We wrote songs and inspired many others to create original pieces through our page The Unreleased Heart.

After leaving Pratapgarh, I thought my writing would stop, but Yuvraj came along with the same likhne ka keeda, and we kept exchanging our works.

Then there was this girl in my coaching (don't remember her name, but she was cute). She was reading a romantic novel by Durjoy Datta. I, being the genius I am, decided to flirt by showing interest in the book instead of her. She gave me the book, unaware that I was more interested in her than the story. But plot twist—I actually got hooked on the novel! That was my first Durjoy Datta read, and it ignited a fire for books, poetry, and open mics.

I was already into rap at the time, and then a rap competition came to my city. I went just to meet Bella and get a pic with him. To prepare for the vibe, I wrote some originals. Who knew that a guy with no intention of competing would land in the top 5?

(P.S.: I did get my picture with Bella!)

A huge thanks to Rekhta Books, especially their Poetic Fusion Combo, for showing me how to represent my thoughts in book form. And to the amazing artists whose illustrations I "borrowed" (okay, fine—stole) from Pinterest—thank you. Hehe. Without your work, this book wouldn't have had the aesthetic vibe it does.

And here's a big shoutout to my brother, Shikhar Gupta, who designed this amazing book cover for me. Haan, itna bheek maangna aur gidgidaana pda wo alag baat hai.

Finally, I owe a special thanks to Akshita (no, not the one mentioned earlier) for playing a pivotal role in motivating me during ***my first book, May I Come In****?. It was just a bucket list thing, but she read the entire book in front of me and said, "You should be proud of your work and spread it more." Those words gave me the confidence I needed to keep writing, and I'll always be grateful for that.*

Lastly, how can I forget ChatGPT? Thanks for translating my quotables into English and handling my grammar struggles.

To everyone who has been a part of my journey—you all have unknowingly encouraged me to keep writing. This book is as much yours as it is mine.

Hello World

Artists perceive the world with a completely different lens.

When most people watch a movie, they focus on the actors, the action, and the drama. But an artist? An artist notices the cinematography, the colour grading, the framing of shots, and the camera movements.

When an artist walks with earphones plugged in, their steps naturally sync to the tempo of the song they're playing.

If these things resonate with you, I'm sorry to say-you have an artist hidden inside you. You can't live a "normal" life. I always say, ***"Creativity is a curse,"*** *because it doesn't let you behave like everyone else.*

Peace comes only when you're doing something productive. If you're idle, you'll feel low and restless.

This book is a result of that restlessness. Late-night scribbles when I couldn't sleep, but my brain was on fire. These are my ideas-and ideas are contagious. Who knows, reading this book might inspire you to write something new too. How cool are we, right? ***We create things that don't even exist yet!***

That's my favourite part about this "curse." In my opinion, it's what makes us truly human.

Art is how we see the world, and it's what separates us from the mundane and mechanical. It's what makes us different from the rigid "Hello World" kind of existence.

See what I did there? A small pun for the programmers in the room. It's not the best, I know, but it popped into my head while typing this, and that's exactly how art works-it's spontaneous, raw, and full of surprises. So, ***I left some blank pages in the book for you guys.*** *Doodle, unleash your thoughts or use it as a shopping list IDGAF. Just* ***make it your own!***

1 se 12 tak school sikhaata hai...
13 se 30 tak zindagi!

1 से 12 तक स्कूल सिखाता है...
13 से 30 तक ज़िंदगी!

School teaches from 1 to 12...
Life teaches from 13 to 30!

Hum tanhaai mei hi theek the
Tere saath aur akelapan hai.

हम तन्हाई में ही ठीक थे,
तेरे साथ और अकेलापन है।

We were fine in solitude,
With you, loneliness feels renewed.

Khuda, aise par de ki sab dekh
hairaan ho jayein,
Phir bhi zameen pe rakh hume, apne
rang na bhool paayein

ख़ुदा, ऐसे पर दे कि सब देख
हैरान हो जाएं,
फिर भी ज़मीन पे रख हमें, अपने
रंग न भूल पाएं।

God, give me wings that leave
all in awe,
But keep me grounded, so I don't
forget who I am for sure.

Iss jacket mein wo baat kahan?
Jo amma ke bune sweater mein
hua karti thi

इस जैकेट में वो बात कहाँ?
जो अम्मा के बुने स्वेटर में हुआ करती
थी

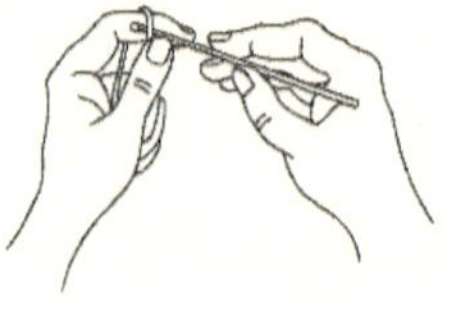

This jacket just doesn't hold the
same charm,
As the sweater mom knitted, so
cozy and warm

Tumhari sundarta mein koi kami
nahi, o saanwli raat,
Meri neend na aane ki wajah,
kisi khushboo ki aadat hai.

तुम्हारी सुंदरता में कोई कमी नहीं,
ओ सांवली रात,
मेरी नींद न आने की वजह,
किसी खुशबू की आदत है।

There's no flaw in your beauty,
oh dusky night,
My sleeplessness is due to a
fragrance's delight

Neend se to roz uth rahe ho...
ye batao, jaagna kab hai?

नींद से तो रोज़ उठ रहे हो...
ये बताओ, जागना कब है?

You wake up from sleep every day...
But tell me, when will you truly awaken?

Zindagi tumne nahi sawaari uski,
Wo to pehle se hi khush thi.
Tum baad mein ghuse!

ज़िंदगी तुमने नहीं सँवारी उसकी,
वो तो पहले से ही खुश थी।
तुम बाद में घुसे!

Her life, you didn't shape or mold,
She was happy, carefree, and bold.
You came in later, truth be told!

Kahin tum galat the,
kahin hum galat the.
Chalo, dono insaan sabit ho gaye.

कहीं तुम गलत थे, कहीं हम गलत थे।
चलो, दोनों इंसान साबित हो गए।

Sometimes you were wrong,
sometimes I was wrong.
Well, looks like we've both proven
to be human all along

Aisi bhi na laga do aadat apni
Ki bin tere
dard se karaahte hi rahein

ऐसी भी ना लगा दो आदत अपनी,
कि बिन तेरे दर्द से कराहते ही रहें।

Don’t make your habit so strong,
That without you,
I keep groaning along.

Thodi khushiyon ka swaad mujhe
bhi lene do,
Gamon ko chakhte-chakhte mann
oob chuka hai mera.

थोड़ी खुशियों का स्वाद मुझे भी लेने दो,
गमों को चखते-चखते मन
ऊब चुका है मेरा।

Let me taste a little bit of
happiness too,
My heart is tired of savoring
sorrows through and through.

Dard to sab dete hain,
Tumne bas thoda kum diya.

दर्द तो सब देते हैं,
तुमने बस थोड़ा कम दिया।

Everyone gives pain,
You just gave a little less.

Hum to tab bhi tumarhe the
Jab tum humarhe nahi the

हम तो तब भी तुम्हारे थे
जब तुम हमारे नहीं थे।

I was yours even then,
When you were never mine.

Jisne apni zindagi mein kabhi gareebi nahi dekhi, wo barbaad hai.

जिसने अपनी ज़िंदगी में कभी गरीबी नहीं देखी, वो बर्बाद है।

Someone who has never seen poverty in their life, is truly lost.

Kaid rehne mein bhi kuch bura nahi
Aadat iski bhi ho jaati hai..

कैद रहने में भी कुछ बुरा नहीं।
आदत इसकी भी हो जाती है।

There's nothing wrong in
being in captivity,
You even get used to it eventually.

Asal mein sirf hum hi
akele reh gaye.
Baakiyon ne to bewafai seekh li!

असल में सिर्फ हम ही अकेले रह गए।
बाकियों ने तो बेवफाई सीख ली।

In truth, I'm the only one left alone,
The rest have mastered the art of
moving on.

Aakhri dafa kab hasa tha??
Jab apno ke saath tha,
Jab apno ka saath tha.

आख़री दफा कब हंसा था?
जब अपनों के साथ था,
जब अपनों का साथ था।

The last time I smiled?
When I was with my own,
When my own stood by me, all the while.

Woh sab kuch kar rahe jo hum
chahte the unse,
bas dard is baat ka hai ki..
kisi aur ke saath.

वो सब कुछ कर रहे जो हम चाहते थे
उनसे, बस दर्द इस बात का है कि...
किसी और के साथ।

They're doing everything I once
wished for,
The pain is just that... it’s with
someone else, not me anymore.

Kyon hai bichane jaal prem ke?
Muska do tum, kaafi hai!

क्यों है बिछाने जाल प्रेम के?
मुस्का दो तुम, काफी है!

Why set the traps of love, my dear?
Just smile, and I'll be
caught right here!

Mat karo naye pyaar ka zikr mujhse,
Kuredna hi hai to kuch
puraane zakhm pde hain!

मत करो नए प्यार का ज़िक्र मुझसे,
कुरेदना ही है तो कुछ पुराने ज़ख्म पड़े
हैं!

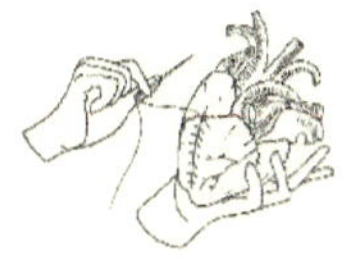

Don't speak to me of new love,
I plea,
If you must dig, there are old
wounds in me!

4 Saal tum zindagi mein the,
Wahi 4 saal zindagi ke the.

4 साल तुम जिंदगी में थे,
वही 4 साल जिंदगी के थे।

Four years you were in my life,
Those same four years were my life.

Bahane mere liye,
waqt auron ke liye,
har kisi ke liye kuch hai uske paas.

बहाने मेरे लिए, वक़्त औरों के लिए,
हर किसी के लिए कुछ है उसके पास।

Excuses for me, time for others.
She has something for everyone.

Imtihaan pyaar ka tha,
hum khoob gye
Itna pyaar diya ki..
wo uub gye

इम्तिहान प्यार का था,
हम खूब गए।
इतना प्यार दिया कि...
वो ऊब गए।

The test of love was here,
I passed with colors clear,
Gave so much love, you see,
That they got bored of me.

Kitni badi saza ek dafa kisi ka
dil dukhaane ki?
Ki ab tak mere tukdon ke
tukde ho rahe hain!

कितनी बड़ी सजा एक दफा किसी का
दिल दुखाने की?
कि अब तक मेरे टुकड़ों के टुकड़े हो
रहे हैं!

How harsh is the punishment for
breaking a heart once?
That even now, my pieces are
breaking into pieces!"

Jaane ke ghum se zayda..
Aane ki umeed takleef deti hai

जाने के ग़म से ज़्यादा...
आने की उम्मीद तकलीफ देती है।

The pain of their absence hurts less...
Than the hope of their return, I confess.

Ab na aaegi baarish
ab na aaega baalam
Jaisa ab tak tha ye ji..
waisa hi rahega aalam

अब न आएगी बारिश,
अब न आएगा बालम
जैसा अब तक था ये जी...
वैसा ही रहेगा आलम।

No rain will come,
no lover will appear,
Life will stay the same,
as it's been till here.

Khafa wo mujhse kya hui,
Mai khafa ab hazaaron se hu

ख़फ़ा वो मुझसे क्या हुई,
मैं ख़फ़ा अब हज़ारों से हूँ।

Upset she got with me, and now,
I’m upset with thousands somehow.

Saath rehna hai to aage Aao na!
Saath rehna na, to aage aao Na!

साथ रहना है तो आगे आओ ना!
साथ रहना ना, तो आगे आओ ना!

If you wish to stay, then come
along!
If you don't, then don't come along!

Mujhe na gum diya kar mujhpe hai
pehle se gum ka bojh
Ye teri baato ko yun yaad krke
rota hu mai roz

मुझे ना ग़म दिया कर,
मुझपे है पहले से ग़म का बोझ,
ये तेरी बातों को यूँ याद करके
रोता हूँ मैं रोज़।

Don't burden me with new sorrows;
I'm already weighed down,
Your words linger in my mind, and I
cry daily, breaking down.

Jb bhi roya, wajah tum thi
Par muskurane ke liye bhi,
tumhe hi dhoondta hu.

जब भी रोया, वजह तुम थी
पर मुस्कुराने के लिए भी..
तुम्हें ही ढूंढता हूँ।

Whenever I cried,
the reason was you,
Yet to smile again, it’s you I pursue.

Aapse pta chale.. to shayad
dard ho hume,
Par kisi aur se pta chala to
beshak toot jaaenge.

आपसे पता चले.. तो शायद
दर्द हो हमें,
पर किसी और से पता चला तो
बेशक टूट जाएंगे।

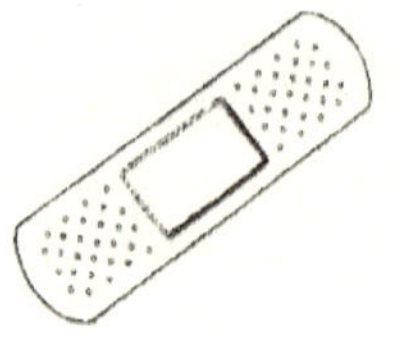

If you find out, maybe
I'll feel the pain,
But if someone else knows,
I'll surely break in vain.

Beech beech mei cheekh deta hu!
log bhul jaate hain ki,
dard hume bhi hota hai.

बीच बीच में चीख देता हूँ!
लोग भूल जाते हैं कि, दर्द हमें भी होता है।

Sometimes I scream out loud,
People forget that I too
feel the pain, unbowed.

Mujhe tanha chhodkar
gairon ko quboolte ho..
Aur phir unn gairon mei tum
mujhko hi dhoondte ho?

मुझे तन्हा छोड़कर गैरों को कबूलते हो..
और फिर उन गैरों में तुम
मुझको ही ढूंढते हो?

You leave me lonely,
accepting others' embrace,
And then in those others,
you still search my face?

Thoda dard to use bhi hua hoga,
dil todne ke liye bhi
patthar hona padta hai.

थोड़ा दर्द तो उसे भी हुआ होगा,
दिल तोड़ने के लिए भी पत्थर होना पड़ता है।

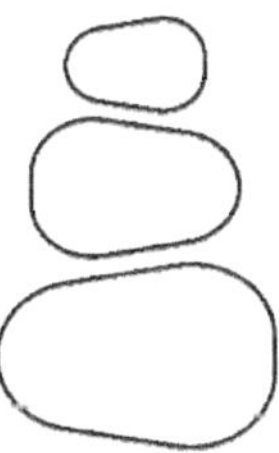

He must have felt some pain too,
To break a heart,
one must be stone too.

Kuch yun dooba hu iss
zindagi ke samadar mei
Na sahara mil raha hai,
na kinara mil raha hai

कुछ यूँ डूबा हूँ इस ज़िंदगी के समंदर में,
ना सहारा मिल रहा है,
ना किनारा मिल रहा है।

Lost so deeply in the ocean of life,
No support in sight,
no shore to survive.

Wafa ki baaton se hain darr chuke
Wafa ke naam pe na jaane
kya kya kar chuke

वफा की बातों से हैं डर चुके,
वफा के नाम पे ना जाने क्या-क्या कर चुके।

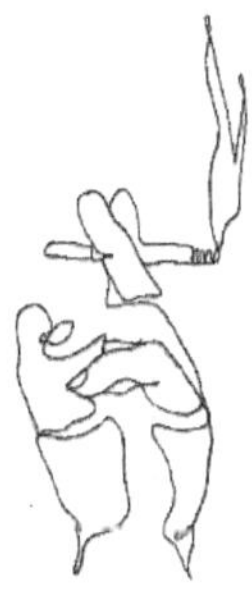

Scared of promises made in loyalty's name,
For loyalty, we've endured endless pain.

Meri galtiyon ko piro kar,
chhodne ki wajah banati ho?
Kuredti ateet bhi ho phir isi bahane,
aur sajaa sunati ho?

मेरी गलतियों को पिरो कर,
छोड़ने की वजह बनाती हो?
कुरेदती अतीत भी हो फिर इसी बहाने,
और सजा सुनाती हो?

You weave my mistakes into
reasons to leave,
Digging up the past,
just to make me grieve?

Ab der karta hu,
kbhi hume bhi jaldi thi
Pyuar mei jo pade,
intezaar karna seekh gaye

अब देर करता हूँ, कभी हमें भी जल्दी थी,
प्यार में जो पड़े, इंतज़ार करना सीख गए।

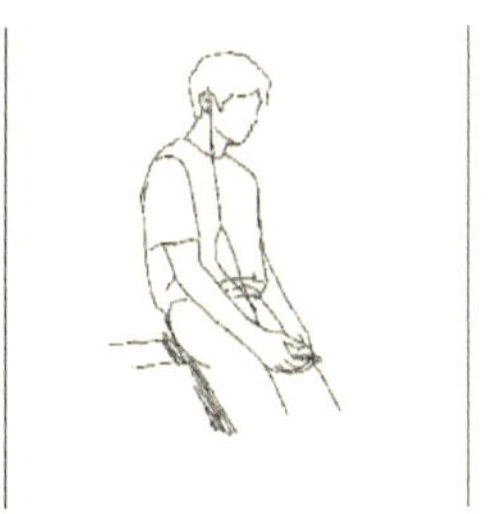

Now I delay, though
once I hurried too,
Falling in love taught me
how to wait, it's true.

Ab meri baaton mei wo
pehli wali baat nahi.

अब मेरी बातों में वो
पहली वाली बात नहीं।

Now in my words, there's no longer
that first spark.

Desh Firangi Ho Jaae
Tum Desi Bankar Naam Karo
Wo Bhasha Chaahe Jo Bolein
Tum Hindi Par Abhimaan Karo

देश फिरंगी हो जाए,
तुम देसी बनकर नाम करो।
वो भाषा चाहे जो बोलें,
तुम हिंदी पर अभिमान करो।

Let the country turn foreign,
You rise as a native,
make your name shine.
No matter what language
they speak,
Hold your pride in Hindi,
it's yours to keep.

Aage badhti duniya se, na jaane
kyun mai rooth raha hu
Is baskin robbins ki bheed mei apne
unn kulfi wale chacha ko
dhoond raha hu

आगे बढ़ती दुनिया से, ना जाने
क्यों मैं रूठ रहा हूँ..
इस बास्किन-रॉबिन्स की भीड़ में, अपने
उन कुल्फी वाले चाचा को ढूंढ रहा हूँ..

Moving forward with the world,
don't know why I'm upset,
In this Baskin-Robbins crowd, I'm
searching for my uncle
with kulfi, you bet.

Laga tha bhul chuka wo beete din,
tod diye wo bandhan..
Par jab kisi naye se judne gaya, to
ehsaas hua ki, purani gaanth to abhi
bhi padi hui hai!
Kholun to kholun kaise?

लगा था भूल चुका वो बीते दिन, तोड़
दिए वो बंधन...
पर जब किसी नए से जुड़ने गया, तो
एहसास हुआ कि, पुरानी गांठ तो अभी
भी पड़ी हुई है!
खोलूं तो खोलूं कैसे?

I thought I had forgotten those past
days, broken those bonds,
But when I tried to connect with
someone new, I realized that there is
still that old knot
how do I even open it?

Aaj farmaaiyish jo aapne
alfaazon ki krdi to
ab ye panne bhrna gawaara hoga,
Hum roz shayari kahenge aur
shayari mei zikr tumarha hoga!

आज फरमाइश जो आपने
अल्फ़ाज़ों की कर दी तो
अब ये पन्ने भरना गवारा होगा,
हम रोज़ शायरी कहेंगे और शायरी में
ज़िक्र तुम्हारा होगा!

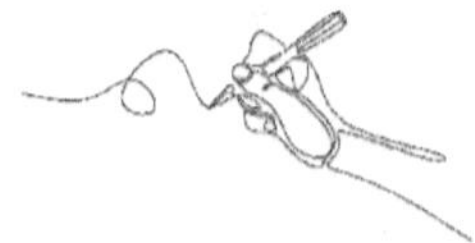

Today you asked for
words to unfold,
Now filling these pages
is a tale untold.
I'll write poetry every single day,
And you'll be the muse in all I say!

Humara sb tumarha hai,
Aur tumarha sb humara!
Poore ki to umeed nahi tumse,
Par aadha bhi mile...to guzaara.

हमारा सब तुम्हारा है,
और तुम्हारा सब हमारा!
पूरे की तो उम्मीद नहीं तुमसे,
पर आधा भी मिले... तो गुज़ारा।

All of mine belongs to you,
And all of yours is mine too.
I don't expect the whole from you,
But even half would
see me through.

Kya hi khalegi kami aapki
kya hi manaenge wo sog
Jinki zindagi mei aapke jaane pe,
haazir hain 10 log

क्या ही खलेगी कमी आपकी,
क्या ही मनाएंगे वो शोक,
जिनकी ज़िंदगी में आपके जाने पे,
हाज़िर हैं 10 लोग।

How will they ever feel
your absence,
how will they mourn your loss,
When even after you're gone,
they still have a crowd to cross.

Na mann tha to aate the kyun?
Wafa ye dikhate the kyun?
Gala ghotna-hi tha pyar ka to
Gale se lagate the kyun?

ना मन था तो आते थे क्यों?
वफ़ा ये दिखाते थे क्यों?
गला घोटना ही था प्यार का तो,
गले से लगाते थे क्यों?

If there was no intent, why did you arrive?
Why show loyalty and make it thrive?
If love was meant to be strangled and torn,
Why hold me close and make me sworn?

Arsa beet gya dekhe tumhe,
Aake apna haal hi sunaate jaate..
Meri tarah kyun tanhaai ka dard na tumhe?
Kuch ni to ye raaz hi batate jaate!

अर्सा बीत गया देखे तुम्हें,
आके अपना हाल ही सुनाते जाते...
मेरी तरह क्यों तन्हाई का दर्द न तुम्हें?
कुछ नहीं तो ये राज़ ही बताते जाते!

It's been ages since I last saw you,
You could've come and shared what you've been through.
Why doesn't loneliness ache in you like it does in me?
If nothing else, you could've revealed this mystery!

Naam lo mera mehfilon mei kabhi,
Naam tumhe tumarha bhi mashoor milega
Palat ke dekh lo panne meri zindagi ke,
Ek baar hi sahi..
zikr tumhaara bhi jarur milega.

नाम लो मेरा महफिलों में कभी,
नाम तुम्हें तुम्हारा भी मशहूर मिलेगा।
पलट के देख लो पन्ने मेरी जिंदगी के,
एक बार ही सही...
ज़िक्र तुम्हारा भी ज़रूर मिलेगा।

Take my name in gatherings someday,
You'll find your name
gaining fame in its way.
Turn the pages of my life and see,
Even once, your mention is bound to be.

Jo tumhara nahi, uspe gumaan kar loge?
Aane ki umeed nahi,
uska intezaar kar loge?
Mohabbat ka izhaar jise
raas nahi aata unse,
Izhaar kiye bagair, pyaar kar loge?

जो तुम्हारा नहीं, उसपे गुमान कर लोगे?
आने की उम्मीद नहीं, उसका इंतज़ार कर लोगे?
मोहब्बत का इज़हार जिसे रास नहीं आता उनसे
इज़हार किए बगैर, प्यार कर लोगे?

Will you take pride in what's not yours to claim?
Wait endlessly for someone who'll never came?
And for the one who shies from love's confession,
Will you love them silently, without expression?

Ek dafa tum ruthoge
aakar tumhe manaunga
Dusri dafa humarhe rishte ko bachaunga
Teesri dafa se pehle na samajh paaunga ki
Chal raha sb ek tarfa kb tk ye chalaunga

एक दफा तुम रूठोगे आकर तुम्हें मनाऊँगा,
दूसरी दफा हमारे रिश्ते को बचाऊँगा।
तीसरी दफा से पहले न समझ पाऊँगा कि,
चल रहा सब एक तरफ़ा, कब तक ये
चलाऊँगा।

Once, you'll sulk, and I'll
make you smile,
Twice, I'll save our bond for a while.
But before the third, I'll start to see,
How long can I run this one-sided spree?

Pooch liya ustad se dil ke,
Dekh ke mera haal batao,
Kyun koi rukta saath na mere,
Kyun mujhko koi jache nahi hai?

Dekh ke mera haal ye dil ka,
Hans ke usne bola mujhse,
"Dil ye sabko kam diya kar,
Zyada tukde bache nahi hain"!

पूछ लिया उस्ताद से दिल के,
देख के मेरा हाल बताओ,
क्यूं कोई रुकता साथ न मेरे,
क्यूं मुझको कोई जचे नहीं है?

देख के मेरा हाल ये दिल का,
हँस के उसने बोला मुझसे,
"दिल ये सबको कम दिया कर
ज़्यादा टुकड़े बचे नहीं हैं"!

I Asked the master of heart,
Seeing my condition, tell me apart,
Why does no one stay with me,
Why don't I like anyone, you see?

Seeing my heart's state, so torn,
He smiled and said, 'You've been worn,
"Give less of your heart, my friend,
There aren't many pieces left to spend."

Until Next Time

Ah! If you're reading this, it means you've either finished the book or you're just skimming to see **"kitna padhna padega?"** Either way, thank you for picking up this book.

Handpicking 50 quotes wasn't easy—I realized that while working on this project. This book is a compilation of my scribbles from the past two years (most of which didn't make the cut). I chose only the ones that still resonated deeply with me, even today.

But let me tell you, there came a point after 47–48 quotes where I hit a wall. My brain froze, and for days, I couldn't come up with anything. Then it hit me—"Arey, mere gaane bhi hain!" So yes, some of the quotables you've read here are taken directly from my tracks. If you enjoyed this book, chances are you'll love my music even more. My entire discography is packed with the same kind of thoughts and one-liners.

Don’t forget to check out my songs and other projects (who knows, you might stumble upon another book from me in the future). And hey, if any page, line, or idea from this book spoke to you, share it on social media and tag me—I’d love to hear what resonated with you and why.

Until next time,

Sayonara! ♥

www.ingramcontent.com/pod-product-compliance
Lightning Source LLC
LaVergne TN
LVHW090132160826
845673LV00017B/2438

* 9 7 9 8 8 9 6 7 3 2 6 0 0 *